Look at all the capes below – these are all the different colours that the woodcutter's wife tried before she decided that red was best. Can you name all the colours she used? Which colour would *you* choose?

blue   yellow   brown   green   pink

Now look at the picture on the opposite page. How many red things can you see?

One day Little Red Riding Hood set out through the forest alone. She was taking a homemade cake and some grape juice to her grandmother, who had a cold

Look at the picture opposite. The grass is growing and the leaves on the trees are green.
Can you guess what season it is, just by looking at the picture? Now look out the window and see how many green things you can see outside.

The picture below shows what happens to the trees as each season comes and goes:

In the winter everything is brown and bare.

In the spring everything is pink and white.

In the fall everything is yellow and orange.

In the summer everything is GREEN!

Which season do you like best?

In a clearing by the side of a little pond, the Big Bad Wolf was waiting!

"Where are you going?" he asked Little Red Riding Hood.

"I'm going to visit my grandmother," she replied. "She has a terrible cold."

Do you know why the water in the pond looks so blue?
Here's a clue: what color is the sky?
That's right - the sky is blue, and the pond is blue because it is reflecting the sky!

On winter days, when the sky is gray, the water in the pond will look grey too. And when little clouds go floating across the sky,
look into the pond and you will see little cloud reflections floating across the water!

Of course, Little Red Riding Hood's favorite color is red, because of her cape, but her *second* favorite color is blue, because it reminds her of the sky on a summer's day.

What is your favorite color, and why?

"Why not take Grandmother some of these pretty
flowers?" suggested the Big Bad Wolf.
So Little Red Riding Hood stopped to pick flowers -
giving the wolf time to run ahead!

Look at all these flowers!
How many flowers do you think Red
Riding Hood has picked? Can you
count them?

Flowers come in
many different
colors.

There are:
red flowers

yellow flowers

pink flowers

purple flowers.

On a piece of
paper, draw a
picture of a flower
and color it in your
favorite color.

Grandmother was sitting up in bed, knitting and sneezing. When she saw the Big Bad Wolf coming, she jumped into the closet to hide.

Grandmother loves bright colors - as you can see! Last year her bedroom was orange, and the year before it was red. This year she has changed it again, and now everything is pink. If you could change the color of your bedroom, which of these colors would you choose?

Grandmother jumped into the closet to hide. Where else could someone hide in Grandmother's bedroom if they saw the Big Bad Wolf coming?

The Big Bad Wolf saw the empty bed and quickly
thought of a plan. He pulled on Grandmother's
nightcap and leaped into Grandmother's warm bed
to wait for Little Red Riding Hood.

Do you know what color the wolf's fur is?

This color is called gray. What other things can you think of that are grey?

Here are some pictures to get you started:

a gray day

gray faucets

gray roofs

gray hair

Did you know that you can make the color gray by adding white to black? The more white you add, the paler the gray becomes.

Look at Grandmother's hairbrush and mirror on the dressing table. Do you know what color they are? When gray is very shiny like this, it is called silver.

Little Red Riding Hood was astonished when she
saw the wolf in bed!
"Grandmother, what huge, hungry eyes you have!"
she said. "And what large, hairy ears! And what
white, pointy teeth!"
At that, the Big Bad Wolf leaped out of bed to eat he

The Big Bad Wolf is very proud of his huge teeth. He brushes them three times a day to keep them so shiny and white. Are your teeth as white as the Big Bad Wolf's teeth? Are your teeth as BIG as the Big Bad Wolf's teeth?

Answer each of the following questions to name five things that are white:

1. What do you go sledding in?
2. What do you put on your cereal in the morning?
3. What do you brush every morning and night to keep them clean?
4. What can you eat fried, scrambled, soft-boiled, or hard-boiled?
5. What floats in the sky on sunny days?

Deep in the forest, the woodcutter was packing up his tools when he heard his daughter's screams.

He grabbed his ax and raced toward Grandmother's house!

Earlier in this book we saw a big blue sky, but now the sun is going down and everything in the forest has turned purple. Look at the purple sunset and the purple shadows. Later, as the sun disappears, the purple will turn to black, and it will be night. Purple is a royal color that used to be worn only by kings. Did you know that you can make the color purple by mixing blue and red together?

Using your finger, trace the path that the woodcutter must take to reach Grandmother's house.

The Big Bad Wolf chased Little Red Riding Hood all around the house, but when he saw the woodcutter's ax, he ran away!
Grandmother came out of the closet. "What a lucky escape!" she cried.

When everybody has calmed down, Grandmother, the woodcutter and Little Red Riding Hood sit down to eat the cake and drink the grape juice. Look at the picture below and answer the following questions:

1. What color is Grandmother's living room?
2. What color is the icing on the cake?
3. What color is the label on the grape juice?
4. What color is Grandmother's apron?

Yellow is the color of sunshine, butter, and buttercups. Grandmother has painted her living room yellow because it makes her think of bright spring days. What color is the living room in your house?

As Little Red Riding Hood and the woodcutter
walked home through the night, the woodcutter
asked: "What lesson have you learned today?"
"I must never talk to strangers in the forest," said
Little Red Riding Hood, and she held tightly to
her father's hand.